PRINCEWILL LAGANG

Blockchain Business: Opportunities for 21st Century Entrepreneurs

First published by PRINCEWILL LAGANG 2023

Copyright © 2023 by Princewill Lagang

All rights reserved. No part of this publication may be reproduced, stored or transmitted in any form or by any means, electronic, mechanical, photocopying, recording, scanning, or otherwise without written permission from the publisher. It is illegal to copy this book, post it to a website, or distribute it by any other means without permission.

Princewill Lagang asserts the moral right to be identified as the author of this work.

First edition

This book was professionally typeset on Reedsy.
Find out more at reedsy.com

Contents

1. Blockchain Business: Opportunities for 21st Century...   1
2. Understanding the Foundations of Blockchain Technology   5
3. Blockchain Business Models: From Cryptocurrencies to Supply...   9
4. Regulatory Considerations in Blockchain Business   14
5. Launching Your Blockchain Business: Strategy, Funding, and...   18
6. Scaling and Growing Your Blockchain Business   23
7. Challenges and Risk Mitigation in the Blockchain Business   28
8. The Future of Blockchain Technology: Opportunities Across...   33
9. Building a Sustainable Blockchain Business   37
10. Conclusion: The Ongoing Journey of Blockchain...   42
11. Resources and Further Reading   46
12. Glossary of Key Blockchain Terms   50
13. Summary   54

1

Blockchain Business: Opportunities for 21st Century Entrepreneurs

In the rapidly evolving landscape of the 21st century, technology has become the cornerstone of innovation and transformation across various industries. One technology, in particular, has gained significant attention and is poised to revolutionize the way we conduct business - blockchain. This chapter serves as a gateway to the world of blockchain, offering a comprehensive exploration of its potential, its impact on entrepreneurship, and the myriad opportunities it presents to forward-thinking individuals in this century.

The Genesis of Blockchain

Before diving into the exciting possibilities of blockchain business, it's essential to understand the origins of this groundbreaking technology. The concept of a blockchain was first introduced by an anonymous person or group known as Satoshi Nakamoto in a whitepaper titled "Bitcoin: A Peer-to-Peer Electronic Cash System" in 2008. The primary purpose of this blockchain was to create a decentralized digital currency, Bitcoin, which eliminated the need for intermediaries like banks and governments to facilitate transactions.

A blockchain is essentially a distributed and immutable ledger that records every transaction ever made on the network. It operates on a decentralized, peer-to-peer network, making it secure, transparent, and resistant to fraud and tampering. The data in a blockchain is organized into blocks, which are cryptographically linked to form a chain. Once a block is added to the chain, it cannot be altered, ensuring the integrity and trustworthiness of the ledger.

The Blockchain Ecosystem

Blockchain technology has evolved far beyond its original use case as a digital currency platform. It has grown into a versatile ecosystem with a multitude of applications, making it an attractive prospect for entrepreneurs. Here's a glimpse of the various aspects of the blockchain ecosystem:

Cryptocurrencies:
   Cryptocurrencies, such as Bitcoin, Ethereum, and Litecoin, have taken the financial world by storm. They serve as a store of value, a medium of exchange, and a unit of account in a borderless, decentralized manner. Cryptocurrencies have not only disrupted traditional financial systems but also created new opportunities for investment and trading.

Smart Contracts:
   Smart contracts are self-executing contracts with the terms of the agreement directly written into code. They automatically execute and enforce the terms without the need for intermediaries, significantly reducing the cost and complexity of legal processes.

Decentralized Finance (DeFi):
   DeFi platforms provide financial services like lending, borrowing, and trading through blockchain technology. They enable users to have greater

control over their finances while minimizing reliance on traditional banks.

Non-Fungible Tokens (NFTs):
NFTs represent unique digital assets, such as art, collectibles, and virtual real estate. They have gained popularity in the world of digital art, gaming, and entertainment, creating new avenues for creators and investors.

Supply Chain Management:
Blockchain technology enhances transparency and traceability in supply chains. It is used to verify the authenticity and origin of products, which is particularly crucial in industries like food, pharmaceuticals, and luxury goods.

Entrepreneurship in the Blockchain Era

The blockchain revolution has unlocked a myriad of opportunities for entrepreneurs, ranging from startups to established businesses. Entrepreneurs who embrace blockchain technology can gain a competitive edge and disrupt industries in the following ways:

Reduced Transaction Costs:
Blockchain enables direct peer-to-peer transactions, eliminating the need for intermediaries and reducing transaction costs. This can be especially beneficial in industries like finance, where fees and delays are common.

Increased Security and Trust:
The immutability and transparency of blockchain make it an ideal tool for securing sensitive information, such as customer data and supply chain records. Entrepreneurs can build trust with their customers by demonstrating their commitment to data security.

Access to Global Markets:
Blockchain enables borderless business operations. Entrepreneurs can

tap into global markets with ease, reaching a broader customer base and diversifying their revenue streams.

Innovations in Existing Business Models:

Existing businesses can integrate blockchain technology to streamline their operations, enhance customer experiences, and explore new revenue streams. For example, loyalty programs, voting systems, and identity verification can all be improved through blockchain.

The Road Ahead

The blockchain revolution is in its early stages, and entrepreneurs who seize the opportunities it offers stand to benefit tremendously. However, navigating this dynamic space requires a deep understanding of the technology, its applications, and the regulatory landscape. This book aims to serve as your guide through the intricate world of blockchain business, helping you unlock its potential, avoid pitfalls, and develop a successful venture in the 21st century.

In the chapters that follow, we will delve into the technical intricacies of blockchain, explore various business use cases, address regulatory considerations, and offer insights into building and scaling your blockchain enterprise. Whether you're a seasoned entrepreneur or a newcomer to the world of business, this book will equip you with the knowledge and tools to thrive in the blockchain era. So, let's embark on this exciting journey and discover the boundless opportunities that blockchain has to offer.

2

Understanding the Foundations of Blockchain Technology

In Chapter 1, we explored the broad landscape of blockchain business opportunities and its potential impact on entrepreneurship in the 21st century. Now, it's time to lay a solid foundation by delving into the fundamental principles of blockchain technology. Understanding these key concepts will be essential as we explore various applications and business models in subsequent chapters.

The Building Blocks of Blockchain

At its core, a blockchain is a distributed ledger composed of interconnected blocks, each containing a list of transactions. To comprehend how this technology works, let's break down the foundational elements:

1. Blocks:
A block is a collection of data, typically a batch of transactions. These transactions can represent various types of digital assets, from cryptocurrencies to digital certificates or even voting records. Each block is encrypted and

linked to the previous block in the chain.

2. Decentralization:
Unlike traditional centralized systems (e.g., banks or government databases), blockchains operate on a decentralized network of computers (nodes). This decentralization ensures that no single entity has complete control over the network, enhancing security and trust.

3. Consensus Mechanisms:
To add a new block to the blockchain, a consensus mechanism is used to validate and agree on the transactions within it. The most common consensus mechanism is Proof of Work (PoW) used in Bitcoin, and Proof of Stake (PoS) used in Ethereum, each with its own approach to reaching consensus.

4. Cryptographic Hashing:
Each block in the blockchain is secured using cryptographic hashes. These one-way mathematical functions create a unique identifier for each block and link it to the previous block, making it virtually impossible to alter data without detection.

5. Immutability:
Once a block is added to the blockchain, it becomes immutable, meaning the data within it cannot be altered or deleted. This immutability is a key feature that ensures the integrity and trustworthiness of the ledger.

How Transactions Are Added to the Blockchain

To better understand how transactions are added to the blockchain, let's walk through a simplified version of the process:

1. Transaction Creation: A user initiates a transaction. This could be sending cryptocurrencies, creating a smart contract, or recording any form of digital data.

UNDERSTANDING THE FOUNDATIONS OF BLOCKCHAIN TECHNOLOGY

2. Transaction Propagation: The transaction is broadcast to the network, where it is picked up by nodes.

3. Verification: Nodes on the network validate the transaction by checking its legitimacy and confirming the user's ownership of the assets involved.

4. Inclusion in a Block: Once verified, the transaction is bundled with other verified transactions into a new block. Miners (in PoW) or validators (in PoS) compete to solve a complex mathematical puzzle, with the first one to succeed earning the right to add the block to the chain.

5. Linking to Previous Block: The new block is linked to the previous block through its cryptographic hash, creating a chain of blocks. This linkage ensures the immutability of data on the blockchain.

6. Broadcasting the Updated Chain: The updated blockchain is then broadcast to all nodes, maintaining a consistent ledger across the entire network.

Types of Blockchains

There are two primary types of blockchains:

1. Public Blockchains:
   Public blockchains, like Bitcoin and Ethereum, are open to anyone, and anyone can participate as a node. They are permissionless and operate on a trustless basis, meaning you don't need to trust any central authority.

2. Private Blockchains:
   Private blockchains, in contrast, are permissioned and typically used by organizations or consortiums. Access is restricted, and participants are known and trusted entities. Private blockchains offer more control but sacrifice some of the trustless and decentralized aspects of public blockchains.

Hybrid and Consortium Blockchains

There are also hybrid and consortium blockchains that blend elements of both public and private blockchains. Hybrid blockchains allow for varying degrees of accessibility and control. Consortium blockchains are usually maintained by a group of organizations rather than a single entity, offering a balance between public and private characteristics.

Conclusion

In this chapter, we've laid the foundation for your understanding of blockchain technology. You now know the key components that make up a blockchain, how transactions are added to the ledger, and the distinctions between public, private, hybrid, and consortium blockchains. With this knowledge in hand, we're ready to explore the diverse range of applications and opportunities that blockchain technology presents for entrepreneurs in the 21st century. In the chapters that follow, we'll delve deeper into these applications and provide practical insights into how to harness the potential of blockchain for your business endeavors.

3

Blockchain Business Models: From Cryptocurrencies to Supply Chain

In the previous chapters, we built a foundational understanding of blockchain technology and its potential for entrepreneurship in the 21st century. Now, it's time to explore the diverse range of business models and applications that are thriving in the blockchain ecosystem. From cryptocurrencies to supply chain management, blockchain technology has opened up countless opportunities for innovative entrepreneurs.

Cryptocurrencies: The Pioneer of Blockchain Business

Cryptocurrencies have been the trailblazers of the blockchain space, with Bitcoin being the most well-known and widely adopted. Bitcoin's success has paved the way for a plethora of alternative cryptocurrencies, each with unique features and use cases.

Use Cases for Cryptocurrencies:

1. Digital Gold: Bitcoin is often referred to as "digital gold" due to its store

of value properties. It serves as a hedge against inflation and economic uncertainty, attracting investors seeking to preserve their wealth.

2. Medium of Exchange: Cryptocurrencies like Bitcoin and Litecoin function as digital cash, enabling fast and secure peer-to-peer transactions, regardless of geographical boundaries.

3. Initial Coin Offerings (ICOs): Blockchain-based startups have raised capital through ICOs, allowing them to issue tokens in exchange for funds. ICOs have disrupted traditional venture capital fundraising.

4. Decentralized Finance (DeFi): DeFi platforms use blockchain technology to create financial services, such as lending, borrowing, and trading, without the need for traditional intermediaries.

Smart Contracts: Automating Business Agreements

Smart contracts are self-executing agreements with the terms of the contract directly written into code. They automate, execute, and enforce agreements, reducing the need for intermediaries and the potential for disputes.

Use Cases for Smart Contracts:

1. Legal Services: Smart contracts can streamline legal processes by automating tasks like wills and estate planning, real estate transactions, and intellectual property agreements.

2. Supply Chain Management: They enhance transparency and traceability in supply chains by automating the verification and recording of product movements.

3. Insurance: Smart contracts can automatically process insurance claims based on predefined conditions, speeding up the claims process and reducing

fraud.

4. Voting Systems: They can be used to create secure and transparent voting systems, making elections more efficient and tamper-resistant.

Decentralized Finance (DeFi): Revolutionizing the Financial Industry

DeFi is a rapidly growing sector within the blockchain space, aiming to decentralize and democratize traditional financial services. It offers opportunities for both users and entrepreneurs to participate in a new, open financial ecosystem.

DeFi Applications:

1. Decentralized Exchanges (DEXs): These platforms allow users to trade cryptocurrencies without relying on centralized exchanges, providing greater security and control.

2. Lending and Borrowing: DeFi platforms enable users to lend their cryptocurrencies and earn interest, or borrow assets by collateralizing their holdings.

3. Stablecoins: Stablecoins are cryptocurrencies designed to maintain a stable value, often pegged to a traditional currency like the US dollar. They provide stability in a volatile crypto market.

4. Yield Farming and Liquidity Provision: Users can provide liquidity to decentralized exchanges and earn rewards, often in the form of interest or tokens.

Non-Fungible Tokens (NFTs): Unique Digital Assets

NFTs have gained significant attention, representing unique digital assets, including digital art, collectibles, virtual real estate, and more. They are stored on blockchains, ensuring their authenticity and ownership.

NFT Use Cases:

1. Digital Art and Collectibles: NFTs have revolutionized the art and collectibles markets, allowing artists and creators to tokenize and sell their work with proven ownership.

2. Gaming: In the gaming industry, NFTs are used to represent in-game items, characters, and virtual real estate, enabling players to trade and own digital assets.

3. Music and Entertainment: Musicians, actors, and content creators are exploring NFTs to monetize their digital content, including music, videos, and virtual experiences.

Supply Chain Management: Ensuring Transparency and Traceability

Blockchain technology enhances transparency and traceability in supply chains, ensuring the authenticity and origin of products. This is particularly vital in industries like food, pharmaceuticals, and luxury goods.

Supply Chain Use Cases:

1. Provenance Tracking: Consumers can trace the origin of products to verify their authenticity and ethical sourcing.

2. Reducing Counterfeits: Blockchain technology can help combat the counterfeiting of luxury goods, pharmaceuticals, and electronics by providing a verifiable history of each item.

3. Sustainability Efforts: Companies can use blockchain to track and verify

sustainability initiatives, such as environmentally-friendly sourcing and production practices.

Conclusion

In this chapter, we've explored a variety of blockchain business models and applications that are thriving in the 21st century. From cryptocurrencies and smart contracts to DeFi, NFTs, and supply chain management, blockchain technology has opened up a wealth of entrepreneurial opportunities. As we continue our journey through the world of blockchain business, we'll delve into practical insights, challenges, and strategies for success in each of these domains. Whether you're a seasoned entrepreneur or just embarking on your business journey, the blockchain ecosystem offers a dynamic landscape to explore and innovate within the ever-evolving digital economy.

4

Regulatory Considerations in Blockchain Business

As we venture further into the world of blockchain business, it is crucial to address the regulatory landscape that surrounds this technology. Blockchain's disruptive potential has captured the attention of governments and regulatory bodies worldwide. In this chapter, we'll explore the various regulatory considerations entrepreneurs must be aware of to navigate the blockchain space successfully.

The Regulatory Landscape

Blockchain operates in a complex regulatory environment, shaped by the unique characteristics of the technology and its various applications. Regulatory frameworks differ from one country to another, and in some cases, even from one state or region to another within the same country. Understanding these regulatory nuances is vital to avoid potential legal issues and compliance challenges.

1. Cryptocurrency Regulations:

Cryptocurrencies, like Bitcoin and Ethereum, are at the forefront of blockchain technology. They have faced varying degrees of regulation globally.

- Money Transmission Laws: In many countries, businesses that deal with cryptocurrencies are subject to money transmitter regulations, which may involve obtaining licenses, conducting Know Your Customer (KYC) and Anti-Money Laundering (AML) checks, and reporting transactions to authorities.

- Securities Regulations: Some countries classify certain cryptocurrencies or token offerings as securities, subjecting them to specific regulations. Understanding the classification of your blockchain-based assets is crucial.

- Taxation: Tax treatment of cryptocurrency transactions varies from place to place. Entrepreneurs must be aware of tax obligations associated with cryptocurrency holdings and transactions in their jurisdiction.

2. Smart Contracts and Legal Recognition:

The legal status of smart contracts, which automate contractual agreements, is a subject of debate. Some jurisdictions recognize them as legally binding, while others require traditional legal agreements alongside smart contracts.

- Digital Signatures: Many countries have implemented digital signature laws that recognize electronic signatures as legally valid, which is essential for the adoption of smart contracts.

3. Decentralized Finance (DeFi) Regulations:

DeFi platforms have disrupted traditional financial services, but their rapid growth has led to increased scrutiny by regulators.

- Licensing and Compliance: DeFi projects that involve lending, borrowing, or trading often fall under existing financial regulations. Licensing and compliance are critical considerations.

4. Initial Coin Offerings (ICOs) and Token Offerings:

ICOs, which are a method of raising capital by issuing tokens, have faced significant regulatory challenges, leading to the emergence of Security Token Offerings (STOs) that aim to comply with securities regulations.

- Securities Laws: Determining whether a token is a security and adhering to securities laws is essential to avoid legal issues.

5. Data Privacy and Identity Regulations:

Blockchain technology stores sensitive data on an immutable ledger, which raises questions about data privacy and identity management.

- General Data Protection Regulation (GDPR): Businesses must ensure they comply with GDPR when dealing with personal data, even if it is stored on a blockchain.

6. Intellectual Property and Patents:

The use of blockchain for intellectual property management and patent systems may require compliance with intellectual property laws.

- Patent Protections: Entrepreneurs looking to protect their blockchain-related inventions may need to file for patents in their jurisdiction.

Global and Local Approaches

Blockchain regulations can vary significantly between countries. Some nations have adopted a proactive approach to embrace and regulate blockchain technology, while others have taken a more cautious or restrictive stance. Entrepreneurs should be aware of the regulatory environment in their region and the regions where they plan to operate.

Navigating the Regulatory Challenges

REGULATORY CONSIDERATIONS IN BLOCKCHAIN BUSINESS

To successfully navigate the regulatory landscape in the blockchain space, entrepreneurs should consider the following strategies:

1. Consult Legal Experts: Engage legal professionals with expertise in blockchain and cryptocurrency regulations to ensure compliance and avoid legal issues.

2. Stay Informed: Keep up-to-date with regulatory changes and developments in the blockchain space. Changes in regulations can impact business operations significantly.

3. Implement KYC and AML Procedures: If your business deals with cryptocurrencies, establish robust Know Your Customer (KYC) and Anti-Money Laundering (AML) procedures to prevent illicit activities and meet regulatory requirements.

4. Operate Transparently: Being transparent about your business operations and financials can help build trust with both regulators and customers.

5. Engage with Regulators: Establish communication channels with regulatory bodies to address concerns and questions, and participate in the regulatory process where appropriate.

Conclusion

As blockchain technology continues to disrupt various industries, it is imperative for entrepreneurs to be well-informed about the regulatory considerations that impact their business ventures. The evolving nature of blockchain regulations underscores the importance of staying up-to-date and working closely with legal experts to ensure compliance with the applicable laws in the regions where you operate. In the next chapter, we'll explore the practical aspects of launching a blockchain business, including funding, team-building, and strategy development.

5

Launching Your Blockchain Business: Strategy, Funding, and Team Building

Having gained insights into the foundations of blockchain technology and the regulatory landscape, it's time to explore the practical aspects of launching your blockchain business. This chapter will guide you through essential considerations such as strategic planning, funding options, and team building.

Strategic Planning for Your Blockchain Business

Successful blockchain businesses begin with a well-thought-out strategy. Whether you're creating a cryptocurrency, a DeFi platform, or a supply chain solution, consider the following strategic elements:

1. Market Analysis:
   - Identify your target market and understand its needs and pain points.
   - Research competitors to discover gaps and opportunities.
   - Evaluate market trends and the demand for blockchain solutions in your chosen sector.

2. Value Proposition:
   - Clearly define the unique value your blockchain solution provides.
   - Focus on how your product or service solves problems and offers benefits to users.

3. Business Model:
   - Determine how you will generate revenue. Common models include transaction fees, subscription-based services, or tokenomics (if launching a cryptocurrency).

4. Technology Stack:
   - Choose the right blockchain platform (e.g., Ethereum, Binance Smart Chain, or build your own) based on your business's specific needs.
   - Select the appropriate development tools and languages.

5. Legal and Regulatory Compliance:
   - Ensure that you understand the regulatory environment in your region and take necessary steps to comply with relevant laws and regulations.

6. Security Measures:
   - Implement robust security protocols to protect your blockchain solution from vulnerabilities and threats.

7. Marketing and User Acquisition:
   - Develop a marketing strategy to reach your target audience.
   - Consider partnerships, influencers, and community engagement to build a user base.

Funding Your Blockchain Venture

Funding is a crucial aspect of launching any business, and blockchain startups are no exception. Here are some funding options to consider:

1. Bootstrapping:
   - Use your own savings and revenue generated by the business to fund its growth.
   - While it requires personal financial commitment, it offers full ownership and control.

2. Angel Investors and Venture Capital:
   - Seek investment from individuals (angel investors) or venture capital firms.
   - They provide funding in exchange for equity, often offering valuable expertise and connections.

3. Initial Coin Offerings (ICOs) or Token Sales:
   - If your business model involves a cryptocurrency or token, consider conducting an ICO or token sale to raise capital.
   - This method allows you to raise funds from a global pool of investors.

4. Security Token Offerings (STOs):
   - If your token is classified as a security, consider conducting an STO, which is compliant with securities regulations.
   - STOs are attractive to investors looking for a regulated investment opportunity.

5. Grants and Contests:
   - Many organizations, both governmental and private, offer grants and prizes for innovative blockchain projects.
   - Research these opportunities and apply for funding or recognition.

6. Crowdfunding:
   - Platforms like Kickstarter or Indiegogo can be used to crowdfund your blockchain project.
   - This approach may work well for consumer-oriented blockchain products.

Building Your Blockchain Team

Your team plays a critical role in the success of your blockchain business. Consider the following when building your team:

1. Technical Expertise:
   - Recruit blockchain developers and experts who understand the technology's intricacies.
   - Ensure your team has experience in the specific blockchain platform you're using.

2. Legal and Regulatory Expertise:
   - Employ legal professionals well-versed in blockchain regulations to help navigate compliance issues.

3. Marketing and Community Management:
   - Building a strong community and effectively marketing your blockchain solution is essential.
   - Hire experts in digital marketing and community management.

4. Cybersecurity Specialists:
   - Blockchain security is paramount. Employ cybersecurity experts to protect your platform against threats.

5. Business and Strategy:
   - A capable business team can help you define a strong strategy and execute it effectively.
   - Look for individuals with experience in startups and business development.

Developing a Minimum Viable Product (MVP)

Before launching your blockchain product or service, consider developing a

Minimum Viable Product (MVP). An MVP is a scaled-down version of your idea that allows you to test your concept, gather user feedback, and make necessary improvements. This approach can save time and resources in the long run.

Conclusion

Launching a blockchain business is an exciting journey, but it requires careful planning and execution. Strategic planning, funding considerations, and building the right team are essential steps on the path to success. Additionally, developing an MVP can help you validate your concept and refine your product or service based on real-world feedback. In the next chapter, we will explore the challenges and opportunities associated with scaling and growing your blockchain business.

6

Scaling and Growing Your Blockchain Business

Congratulations on making it this far in your journey to launch and establish a blockchain business. In this chapter, we will explore the strategies and considerations for scaling and growing your blockchain venture, whether it's a cryptocurrency, DeFi platform, NFT marketplace, or any other blockchain-based business.

The Growth Trajectory

Scaling a blockchain business can be a complex and challenging process. It often involves expanding your user base, increasing revenue, and optimizing your operations. Here are key factors to consider as you scale your blockchain business:

1. User Adoption and Community Building:
    - Continually focus on user acquisition and retention.
    - Foster an active and engaged community around your blockchain project.
    - Implement marketing and user acquisition strategies that resonate with

your target audience.

2. Expanding Use Cases:
   - Explore additional use cases for your blockchain technology. Consider diversifying into related industries or applications.
   - For example, if you started with a cryptocurrency, you might consider expanding into DeFi or NFTs.

3. International Expansion:
   - Assess the feasibility of expanding your business to international markets.
   - Be aware of regulatory variations and adapt your strategy accordingly.

4. Technology Enhancements:
   - Continuously improve your blockchain technology by optimizing scalability, security, and performance.
   - Stay updated with the latest developments in blockchain to remain competitive.

5. Compliance and Regulations:
   - As you grow, navigate the evolving regulatory landscape, ensuring your business complies with local and global regulations.
   - Seek legal counsel to guide your compliance efforts.

6. Security and Risk Management:
   - As your business becomes more attractive to potential attackers, invest in cybersecurity and risk management.
   - Stay vigilant against potential threats and vulnerabilities.

Funding for Growth

To finance the growth of your blockchain business, consider various funding options:

SCALING AND GROWING YOUR BLOCKCHAIN BUSINESS

1. Revenue and Profits:
   - Reinvest revenue generated by your business to fund expansion.
   - Focus on optimizing your operations to increase profitability.

2. Venture Capital and Equity Funding:
   - Explore opportunities to raise capital from venture capitalists or equity investors to support your growth initiatives.
   - Prepare a compelling pitch and business plan to attract investment.

3. Token Sales and Funding Rounds:
   - If you operate a cryptocurrency or blockchain project, you may consider additional token sales or funding rounds to secure capital.
   - These can be used for technology development, marketing, and user acquisition.

Partnerships and Collaborations

Forming strategic partnerships and collaborations can provide a significant boost to your blockchain business. Consider the following:

1. Industry Partnerships:
   - Collaborate with other businesses in your industry to offer complementary services or share resources.
   - These partnerships can help you tap into new markets and customer bases.

2. Developer and Ecosystem Partnerships:
   - Engage with other blockchain projects or developers to create interoperability and a broader ecosystem.
   - This can enhance the value proposition of your blockchain solution.

3. Integration Partnerships:
   - Partner with established platforms or services to integrate your blockchain

technology.
   - Integration can expand your reach and user base.

Building a Strong Brand and Reputation

A strong brand and positive reputation are essential assets as you scale your blockchain business. Here's how to build and maintain them:

1. Consistency:
   - Ensure a consistent and clear message across all your communication channels.
   - Consistency builds trust and recognition.

2. Customer Support:
   - Prioritize excellent customer support to address user inquiries and issues promptly.
   - Positive interactions with customers can enhance your reputation.

3. Transparency:
   - Be transparent about your business operations, updates, and any challenges you face.
   - Transparency fosters trust and loyalty.

Conclusion

Scaling and growing your blockchain business is an exciting and challenging phase of your entrepreneurial journey. To succeed, focus on user adoption, international expansion, technological enhancements, and compliance. Utilize funding options to finance your growth and consider strategic partnerships and collaborations to expand your reach. A strong brand and positive reputation will underpin your growth efforts, so prioritize transparency, consistency, and top-notch customer support. In the next chapter, we will explore the potential challenges and risks in the blockchain business space and provide insights on how to mitigate them.

7

Challenges and Risk Mitigation in the Blockchain Business

The blockchain business space offers numerous opportunities, but it also presents unique challenges and risks. In this chapter, we will explore some of the most common challenges faced by blockchain entrepreneurs and provide insights on how to mitigate these risks effectively.

Regulatory Uncertainty

Challenge: The regulatory landscape for blockchain and cryptocurrencies varies widely from one region to another, and it continues to evolve. The lack of clear and consistent regulations can create uncertainty and compliance challenges for blockchain businesses.

Mitigation:
  - Engage with legal experts who specialize in blockchain regulations to stay informed and navigate evolving laws.
  - Design your business model with flexibility to adapt to changing regulations.

- Seek licenses or approvals where necessary to ensure compliance with existing laws.

Security Vulnerabilities

Challenge: Blockchain is not immune to security threats. Vulnerabilities in smart contracts, wallet hacks, and other breaches can lead to significant financial losses and damage your business's reputation.

Mitigation:
- Prioritize security by conducting regular security audits and penetration testing.
- Implement robust authentication, encryption, and access control measures.
- Educate your team and users about best security practices.

Market Volatility

Challenge: The cryptocurrency market is highly volatile. The value of digital assets can fluctuate significantly in a short period, impacting your business's financial stability.

Mitigation:
- Diversify your assets and holdings to reduce risk.
- Use risk management strategies such as stop-loss orders and portfolio rebalancing.
- Maintain a long-term perspective and avoid making impulsive decisions based on short-term price fluctuations.

Technology Scalability

Challenge: As your blockchain business grows, you may encounter scalability issues, such as slow transaction processing times and network congestion.

Mitigation:
- Choose a blockchain platform with proven scalability solutions.
- Monitor network performance and adapt your technology stack as needed.
- Collaborate with experienced developers and experts in blockchain scalability.

Intellectual Property and Patents

Challenge: Blockchain innovation often involves new technologies and processes. Without proper protection, your intellectual property may be vulnerable to infringement.

Mitigation:
- Consider applying for patents to protect your blockchain-related inventions.
- Draft clear and enforceable contracts with partners, developers, and employees to protect your intellectual property.
- Be vigilant about potential infringements and take legal action if necessary.

Competition

Challenge: The blockchain space is highly competitive, with numerous projects and businesses vying for users' attention and investment.

Mitigation:
- Differentiate your business by offering unique features, better user experiences, or enhanced security.
- Build a strong brand and community to foster loyalty among users.
- Continuously innovate and adapt to market trends and changing user preferences.

Token Price and Market Sentiment

Challenge: The performance and sentiment of your cryptocurrency or token can significantly impact your business. A declining token price or negative market sentiment can affect user confidence and project viability.

Mitigation:
- Develop a transparent and clear roadmap to instill confidence in your project.
- Focus on building real utility and value for your token beyond speculative trading.
- Communicate effectively with your community to manage expectations during market fluctuations.

Lack of Awareness and Adoption

Challenge: Educating users and businesses about the value and benefits of blockchain technology can be challenging, especially in sectors unfamiliar with its potential.

Mitigation:
- Invest in educational content and marketing to raise awareness about your blockchain solution.
- Collaborate with industry partners and associations to advocate for blockchain adoption.
- Provide user-friendly interfaces and guides to facilitate adoption.

Conclusion

The blockchain business space offers great promise, but it also comes with challenges and risks. By understanding these challenges and implementing effective mitigation strategies, you can increase the likelihood of success in your blockchain venture. Keep in mind that the blockchain landscape is dynamic, so staying informed, adaptable, and proactive is essential to navigate the ever-evolving environment successfully.

In the next chapter, we will explore the future of blockchain technology and its potential impact on various industries, shedding light on the opportunities that lie ahead for entrepreneurs in the 21st century.

8

The Future of Blockchain Technology: Opportunities Across Industries

As we look ahead to the future of blockchain technology, we find a landscape teeming with opportunities that promise to reshape numerous industries. In this chapter, we'll explore the potential impact of blockchain on various sectors, uncovering opportunities that entrepreneurs can leverage in the 21st century.

Healthcare and Medical Records

Opportunity: Blockchain can revolutionize the healthcare sector by providing secure and interoperable medical records. Patients can have complete control over their health data, granting access only to authorized healthcare providers.

Benefits: Enhanced data security, streamlined access to patient information, reduced administrative costs, and improved patient outcomes.

Supply Chain Management

Opportunity: Blockchain's transparency and traceability features are poised to transform supply chain management. From food to luxury goods, blockchain can provide end-to-end visibility, reducing fraud and ensuring product authenticity.

Benefits: Reduced counterfeits, improved quality control, faster recalls, and more sustainable supply chains.

Real Estate and Property Management

Opportunity: Blockchain simplifies property transactions through smart contracts and tokenization. It enables fractional ownership and makes real estate investment accessible to a broader audience.

Benefits: Faster and more efficient transactions, reduced paperwork, lower costs, and improved liquidity.

Energy and Sustainability

Opportunity: Blockchain can underpin energy markets, allowing for peer-to-peer energy trading, carbon credit markets, and transparent tracking of renewable energy sources.

Benefits: Reduced energy waste, cost savings, increased adoption of renewable energy, and a more sustainable planet.

Education and Credential Verification

Opportunity: Blockchain can verify and store educational credentials, certificates, and diplomas, reducing fraud and improving the hiring process for employers and institutions.

Benefits: Enhanced trust in educational credentials, simplified verification, and improved job matching.

Voting and E-Government

Opportunity: Blockchain can enable secure and transparent digital voting systems, reducing fraud and increasing voter participation.

Benefits: Improved electoral integrity, faster vote counting, and greater accessibility for voters.

Intellectual Property and Content Creation

Opportunity: Blockchain can protect intellectual property rights and enable creators to manage and monetize their digital content through NFTs.

Benefits: Increased protection for content creators, fair compensation, and new monetization opportunities.

Cross-Border Payments

Opportunity: Blockchain-based cross-border payment systems can offer faster, cheaper, and more transparent international money transfers, especially for the unbanked and underbanked.

Benefits: Reduced transaction costs, faster settlements, financial inclusion, and remittances with lower fees.

Agriculture and Food Safety

Opportunity: Blockchain can trace the journey of food products from farm to table, improving food safety, reducing fraud, and enhancing supply chain efficiency.

Benefits: Enhanced food safety, reduced food waste, and increased trust in the food supply chain.

Entertainment and Gaming

Opportunity: NFTs and blockchain technology are transforming the entertainment and gaming industries. NFTs enable ownership of digital assets, creating new revenue streams for creators and immersive experiences for users.

Benefits: New monetization models, enhanced user engagement, and opportunities for content creators.

Autonomous Organizations

Opportunity: Decentralized autonomous organizations (DAOs) run on blockchain, allowing for transparent and automated decision-making processes.

Benefits: Reduced bureaucracy, enhanced transparency, and community-driven governance.

Conclusion

The future of blockchain technology is marked by vast opportunities across various industries. Entrepreneurs in the 21st century have the chance to leverage blockchain to disrupt traditional systems, increase transparency, and improve efficiency. As we move forward, it's crucial to stay updated with the latest blockchain developments and to explore the potential of this transformative technology in your field of interest. The blockchain journey is still unfolding, and the entrepreneurs of today have the chance to shape the industries of tomorrow.

9

Building a Sustainable Blockchain Business

Creating and growing a sustainable blockchain business is a multifaceted endeavor that requires strategic planning, resilience, and a long-term perspective. In this chapter, we'll explore the key elements of building a sustainable blockchain business that can thrive in the evolving digital landscape.

Long-Term Vision

A sustainable blockchain business starts with a clear and compelling long-term vision. Your vision should encompass the following aspects:

- Mission Statement: Define the core purpose and values of your blockchain business.
    - Market Opportunity: Identify the market problems you aim to solve or the opportunities you want to seize.
    - Value Proposition: Describe the unique value your blockchain solution offers to users.

- Impact Goals: Articulate the positive impact you aim to have on your industry, society, and the environment.

Customer-Centric Approach

A sustainable business prioritizes its customers. Keep these principles in mind:

- User Experience: Focus on providing a seamless and intuitive user experience to keep your customers engaged and satisfied.
    - Feedback Loop: Establish channels for users to provide feedback, and use this input to improve your blockchain product or service.
    - Responsive Support: Offer responsive customer support to address user concerns and inquiries promptly.

Financial Stability

Financial stability is crucial for long-term sustainability. Ensure that your blockchain business has solid financial foundations:

- Revenue Streams: Diversify revenue sources to reduce reliance on a single income stream.
    - Budget Management: Maintain a disciplined approach to budgeting, tracking expenses, and managing cash flow.
    - Investment and Capital: Secure funding when necessary to fuel growth and development.

Regulatory Compliance

Stay compliant with local and international regulations to ensure your business remains in good standing:

- Legal Counsel: Engage with legal experts who understand blockchain

regulations to navigate the evolving landscape.
- Transparency: Be transparent about your compliance efforts to instill trust in users and regulators.
- Adaptability: Prepare to adjust your business model or practices in response to regulatory changes.

Team Building and Development

Your team is a vital asset for a sustainable blockchain business:

- Talent Acquisition: Continuously recruit and retain top talent in blockchain development, marketing, compliance, and other essential areas.
- Training and Development: Invest in ongoing training to keep your team updated with the latest blockchain trends and technology.
- Collaboration: Foster a collaborative and innovative work environment that encourages team members to share ideas and solutions.

Ecosystem and Partnerships

Leverage the blockchain ecosystem and form strategic partnerships to support your growth:

- Ecosystem Engagement: Engage with other blockchain projects and communities to create a network of like-minded organizations.
- Strategic Alliances: Form strategic partnerships with companies and organizations that complement your business goals.
- Industry Involvement: Participate in industry associations and standards-setting bodies to influence the future of blockchain in your sector.

Technology and Innovation

Maintain a focus on technological innovation to keep your blockchain business competitive:

- Research and Development: Allocate resources to research and develop new features or solutions that address emerging industry needs.
- Tech Stack Maintenance: Stay updated with the latest advancements in blockchain technology and upgrade your tech stack accordingly.
- Security Measures: Prioritize cybersecurity to protect your blockchain solution from vulnerabilities and threats.

Community Building and Engagement

Building and nurturing a community around your blockchain business can contribute to sustainability:

- Community Management: Employ community managers to engage with users, answer questions, and facilitate discussions.
- Communication Channels: Maintain a strong online presence through social media, forums, and newsletters to keep the community informed.
- Transparency: Share updates and progress with your community to build trust and loyalty.

Environmental and Social Responsibility

Sustainable businesses consider their impact on the environment and society:

- Environmental Practices: Implement eco-friendly practices and consider the environmental impact of your operations.
- Social Initiatives: Participate in or initiate social responsibility programs to give back to the community and support charitable causes.

Conclusion

Building a sustainable blockchain business is a journey that involves careful planning, ongoing adaptation, and a commitment to your long-term vision. As the blockchain ecosystem continues to evolve, staying true to your mission and values while maintaining a customer-centric approach will be instrumental in your success. By embracing innovation, nurturing your team, and contributing positively to society and the environment, you can create a blockchain business that thrives well into the future.

10

Conclusion: The Ongoing Journey of Blockchain Entrepreneurship

As we conclude this guide on blockchain entrepreneurship, it's important to recognize that the journey of building and growing a blockchain business is ongoing. The dynamic nature of blockchain technology and the ever-evolving digital landscape ensure that there will always be new challenges and opportunities to explore. In this final chapter, we'll reflect on the key takeaways and provide some parting advice for aspiring blockchain entrepreneurs.

Key Takeaways

1. Education is Empowerment: Blockchain technology is complex and rapidly evolving. Continuous learning and staying updated with industry developments are crucial for success in this field.

2. Diversity of Opportunities: Blockchain technology offers a diverse range of opportunities, from cryptocurrencies and smart contracts to NFTs, supply chain solutions, and more. The key is to find the niche that aligns with your

passion and expertise.

3. Regulatory Awareness: Regulations in the blockchain space are still developing. Staying informed about the regulatory environment in your region and engaging with legal experts is essential.

4. Security is Paramount: Protecting your blockchain solution and the assets it manages is non-negotiable. Prioritize security measures, conduct audits, and stay vigilant against threats.

5. User-Centric Approach: User experience and community building are fundamental. Listen to your users, provide excellent support, and foster a strong community around your blockchain project.

6. Long-Term Vision: Having a clear and compelling long-term vision, grounded in your mission and values, is essential for guiding your business through challenges and opportunities.

7. Adaptability and Innovation: The blockchain landscape is ever-changing. Your business must remain adaptable and innovative to stay competitive and relevant.

8. Ethical Responsibility: Consider the ethical and environmental impact of your blockchain business. Social and environmental responsibility is increasingly important to consumers and investors.

Parting Advice

As you embark on your journey as a blockchain entrepreneur, here are some parting words of advice:

1. Embrace Uncertainty: The blockchain space is inherently uncertain. Be prepared to navigate unexpected challenges and seize new opportunities as

they arise.

2. Build a Network: Collaborate with peers, mentors, and industry experts. Your network can provide valuable insights and support.

3. Persistence is Key: Building a successful blockchain business can be challenging, and setbacks are common. Persistence and resilience are your allies.

4. Balance Innovation and Risk Management: While innovation is critical, balance it with risk management and compliance to maintain long-term sustainability.

5. Stay True to Your Vision: Your long-term vision and mission should guide your decision-making. Let them be the North Star for your blockchain journey.

6. Never Stop Learning: The blockchain ecosystem is constantly evolving. Keep learning, exploring, and adapting to remain at the forefront of this dynamic field.

7. Celebrate Successes: Celebrate your achievements, no matter how small they may seem. Recognizing milestones is essential for motivation and morale.

8. Contribute to the Ecosystem: Give back to the blockchain community by sharing knowledge, supporting open-source projects, and participating in initiatives that advance the technology.

The blockchain journey is a testament to the power of innovation, entrepreneurship, and the potential for transformative change. It is a journey that will continue to shape industries and redefine the digital landscape for years to come. As a blockchain entrepreneur, you have the opportunity to be at the forefront of this evolution, to create meaningful impact, and to leave a lasting legacy in the 21st century digital economy. Embrace this journey with passion, dedication, and a commitment to excellence. Your contributions to the blockchain space have the potential to shape the future in remarkable ways.

11

Resources and Further Reading

As you continue your journey in the world of blockchain entrepreneurship, it's essential to stay informed and well-equipped with knowledge and resources. In this final chapter, we provide a list of recommended resources and further reading to help you explore blockchain technology, keep up with the latest developments, and deepen your understanding of this dynamic field.

Books

1. "Mastering Bitcoin" by Andreas M. Antonopoulos: A comprehensive guide to understanding Bitcoin, its technology, and its impact on the financial world.

2. "Blockchain Basics: A Non-Technical Introduction in 25 Steps" by Daniel Drescher: An accessible introduction to the fundamental concepts of blockchain technology.

3. "Crypto" by Steven Levy: This book explores the history and impact of cryptocurrency, from Bitcoin's early days to its role in shaping the financial

industry.

4. "Blockchain Revolution" by Don Tapscott and Alex Tapscott: An exploration of how blockchain technology is transforming various industries beyond finance.

5. "The Basics of Bitcoins and Blockchains" by Antony Lewis: A beginner-friendly guide that covers the fundamentals of Bitcoin, blockchain, and cryptocurrencies.

Websites and Blogs

1. [Coindesk](https://www.coindesk.com): A leading cryptocurrency and blockchain news source with in-depth analysis and insights.

2. [Cointelegraph](https://cointelegraph.com): Another reputable cryptocurrency news site covering a wide range of blockchain-related topics.

3. [Blockchain at Berkeley](https://blockchain.berkeley.edu): The educational arm of UC Berkeley that offers a wealth of blockchain resources and research.

4. [Consensys Blog](https://consensys.net/blog/): Consensys is a blockchain software technology company, and their blog provides valuable insights into blockchain technology.

5. [Ethereum Blog](https://blog.ethereum.org): For updates and in-depth information about Ethereum and its ecosystem.

Online Courses and Tutorials

1. [Coursera](https://www.coursera.org): Offers a variety of blockchain-related courses from top universities and institutions.

2. [edX](https://www.edx.org): Provides blockchain courses and certifications from universities and organizations around the world.

3. [Udemy](https://www.udemy.com): Offers a wide range of blockchain courses, from introductory to advanced levels.

Podcasts

1. [Unchained](https://unchainedpodcast.com): Hosted by Laura Shin, this podcast explores the world of blockchain and cryptocurrencies through in-depth interviews with industry experts.

2. [Epicenter](https://epicenter.tv): A weekly podcast that covers blockchain, cryptocurrencies, and the decentralized web.

3. [The Pomp Podcast](https://anthonypompliano.com): Hosted by Anthony "Pomp" Pompliano, this podcast features discussions with influential figures in the blockchain and crypto space.

Forums and Communities

1. [BitcoinTalk](https://bitcointalk.org): One of the oldest and most active forums for discussions related to Bitcoin and cryptocurrencies.

2. [Reddit r/ethereum](https://www.reddit.com/r/ethereum/): A Reddit community dedicated to Ethereum, with discussions about development, news, and projects.

3. [Crypto Twitter](https://twitter.com): Many prominent figures and experts in the blockchain space share insights and updates on Twitter.

Research Papers and Whitepapers

RESOURCES AND FURTHER READING

1. [Bitcoin Whitepaper](https://bitcoin.org/bitcoin.pdf): Satoshi Nakamoto's original whitepaper that introduced Bitcoin.

2. [Ethereum Whitepaper](https://ethereum.org/whitepaper/): Vitalik Buterin's whitepaper that outlines the Ethereum blockchain platform.

3. [Libra Whitepaper](https://libra.org/en-US/white-paper/): The whitepaper for Facebook's cryptocurrency project (now known as Diem).

4. [Google Scholar](https://scholar.google.com): A resource for academic research papers and articles related to blockchain technology.

These resources will serve as valuable references and learning materials as you continue your journey in the blockchain space. Remember that the blockchain ecosystem is ever-evolving, so staying informed and engaged with the community is key to success in this dynamic field. Good luck in your blockchain entrepreneurship endeavors, and may you contribute to the ongoing transformation of the digital landscape in meaningful ways.

12

Glossary of Key Blockchain Terms

Blockchain technology comes with its own unique terminology and jargon. This glossary provides definitions for key terms and phrases commonly used in the blockchain and cryptocurrency space:

1. Blockchain: A distributed ledger technology that records transactions in a secure and immutable manner. It consists of a chain of blocks, each containing a set of transactions.

2. Cryptocurrency: A digital or virtual currency that uses cryptography for security. Examples include Bitcoin, Ethereum, and Litecoin.

3. Decentralization: The distribution of control, authority, and data across a network of nodes rather than relying on a central authority or server.

4. Node: A device or computer that participates in the blockchain network, validating and relaying transactions and maintaining a copy of the blockchain.

5. Consensus Mechanism: A protocol or algorithm used to achieve agreement among network nodes regarding the validity of transactions. Common

GLOSSARY OF KEY BLOCKCHAIN TERMS

mechanisms include Proof of Work (PoW) and Proof of Stake (PoS).

6. Smart Contract: Self-executing contracts with the terms of the agreement directly written into code. They automatically execute and enforce contract terms upon specific conditions being met.

7. Mining: The process by which new cryptocurrency coins are created and transactions are added to the blockchain. Miners solve complex mathematical puzzles to validate and add blocks.

8. Wallet: A digital tool for storing, sending, and receiving cryptocurrencies. Wallets can be software-based (online, mobile) or hardware-based (physical devices).

9. Private Key: A cryptographic key known only to the wallet owner, used to sign transactions and access cryptocurrency holdings.

10. Public Key: A cryptographic key associated with a wallet's address, used to verify digital signatures and receive funds.

11. Address: A string of characters that represents a location on the blockchain where cryptocurrency can be sent. It is derived from the public key.

12. Token: A digital asset or representation of an asset or utility on a blockchain. Tokens can have various use cases, including serving as digital currencies, access keys, or assets in decentralized applications.

13. Initial Coin Offering (ICO): A method of fundraising in which new cryptocurrency tokens are sold to investors before they are listed on exchanges.

14. Altcoin: Any cryptocurrency other than Bitcoin. Examples include

Ethereum, Ripple, and Litecoin.

15. Fork: A split or divergence in the blockchain's history resulting from changes in the underlying protocol. Forks can be hard forks (irreversible) or soft forks (compatible with previous versions).

16. Consensus Fork: A change in the consensus rules of a blockchain network. It can be contentious and lead to a network split.

17. Tokenomics: The economic and incentive structure of a blockchain or cryptocurrency, including the distribution and supply of tokens.

18. DeFi (Decentralized Finance): A set of financial services and applications built on blockchain technology that aim to replace traditional financial intermediaries.

19. NFT (Non-Fungible Token): A unique digital token representing ownership of a specific, non-interchangeable item or piece of content, often used in digital art and collectibles.

20. Oracles: Systems or services that provide real-world data to smart contracts on the blockchain. They help smart contracts make decisions based on external information.

21. Whitepaper: A formal document that outlines the concept, technology, and potential impact of a blockchain project or cryptocurrency.

22. Immutable: A property of blockchain data indicating that once recorded, transactions or blocks cannot be altered or deleted.

23. Permissioned Blockchain: A blockchain network where participants are restricted and require permission to join, typically used in enterprise applications.

24. Gas (or Transaction Fee): The fee paid to miners for processing transactions on the blockchain. It helps prevent network abuse and congestion.

25. Cold Storage: A method of storing cryptocurrencies offline, typically on hardware wallets or paper wallets, to protect them from online threats.

26. Sharding: A technique to improve blockchain scalability by breaking the network into smaller, more manageable segments (shards) that process transactions independently.

27. ATH (All-Time High): The highest price level ever reached by a cryptocurrency in its trading history.

28. DYOR (Do Your Own Research): An admonition to conduct thorough research and due diligence before investing in or using cryptocurrencies.

This glossary provides a foundation for understanding blockchain-related terminology. It's important to keep learning and stay updated as the blockchain space evolves, as new terms and concepts continue to emerge.

13

Summary

In this comprehensive guide on blockchain entrepreneurship, we've explored the world of blockchain technology and its impact on the business landscape. Here's a summary of the key chapters:

1. Introduction: We began by introducing the concept of blockchain technology and its transformative potential for entrepreneurs in the 21st century.

2. Blockchain Basics: This chapter provided a foundational understanding of blockchain technology, including its core principles and components.

3. Blockchain Business Ideas: We delved into a wide range of blockchain business ideas, from cryptocurrencies to decentralized applications (DApps) and beyond.

4. Starting Your Blockchain Business: This chapter outlined the essential steps for launching a blockchain business, from idea generation to product development and funding.

5. Legal and Regulatory Considerations: We discussed the importance of understanding the legal and regulatory landscape when operating in the

SUMMARY

blockchain space.

6. Scaling and Growing Your Blockchain Business: This chapter explored strategies for scaling and expanding your blockchain venture, focusing on user adoption, international expansion, and more.

7. Challenges and Risk Mitigation: We identified common challenges and risks faced by blockchain entrepreneurs and provided insights on how to mitigate them effectively.

8. The Future of Blockchain Technology: This chapter explored the potential impact of blockchain in various industries, from healthcare to voting systems, highlighting opportunities for entrepreneurs.

9. Building a Sustainable Blockchain Business: We discussed the elements essential for building a sustainable blockchain business, including long-term vision, financial stability, and ethical responsibility.

10. Conclusion: In the final chapter, we offered parting advice to aspiring blockchain entrepreneurs, emphasizing the need for ongoing learning, adaptability, and ethical responsibility.

11. Resources and Further Reading: This chapter provided a list of recommended resources, including books, websites, podcasts, and forums, to help entrepreneurs stay informed and engaged with the blockchain community.

12. Glossary: A comprehensive glossary of key blockchain terms to aid in understanding the unique language and concepts of blockchain technology.

This guide serves as a valuable resource for individuals looking to embark on a journey in blockchain entrepreneurship, offering insights, practical advice, and a strong foundational knowledge of blockchain technology and its applications. As the blockchain ecosystem continues to evolve, staying informed, adaptable, and committed to innovation is essential for success in this dynamic field.

www.ingramcontent.com/pod-product-compliance
Lightning Source LLC
LaVergne TN
LVHW010435070526
838199LV00066B/6028